A Star to Guide Me

Illustrated Prayers for Children

Illustrations by Ruthild Busch-Schumann

Floris Books

The moon shines bright,
The stars give light
Before the break of day.
God bless you all,
Both big and small,
And send a happy day.

A gift for

Esme
on your christening
From day.

Wendy & Gerard
much love
x

Now, before I run and play,
Don't let me forget to pray
To God who kept me safe all night
And woke me with the morning light.
Help me, Lord, to love you more
Than I have ever loved before.
In my work and in my play,
Please be with me through the day.

I awaken every morning
To the glory of the sun,
And the sunlight touches me
And the hearts of everyone,
And I lift up my heart
To the glory of the sun.

I awaken every morning
To the songbirds in the sky,
And I hear their lovely song
As along their way they fly,
And in my heart I rise
With the songbirds in the sky.

I awaken every morning
To the people that I know,
And I see in their eyes
All the love and care they show,
And I hold in my heart
All the people that I know.

Trevor Smith Westgarth

$\mathcal{B}e$ like a bright flame before me,
Be like a guiding star above me,
Be like a smooth path below me,
Be like a kind shepherd behind me,
Today, tonight and for ever.

Based on 'The Guardian Angel', Carmina Gadelica

Thank you, Lord, for happy hearts,
For rain and sunny weather.
Thank you, Lord, for this food,
And that we are together.

Over the earth is a blanket of green,
Over the green is the dew,
Over the dew are the waving trees,
Over the trees is the blue.
Across the blue are the racing clouds,
Over the clouds is the sun,
Over it all is the love of God,
Blessing us every one.

Thank you, God in heaven,
For a day begun.
Thank you for the breezes,
Thank you for the sun.
For this time of happiness,
For our work and play,
Thank you, God in heaven,
For another day.

Thank you for the food we eat,
Thank you for the friends we meet,
Thank you for the birds that sing,
Thank you, God, for everything.

Give praise to God for brother Sun,
Who makes our day so bright;
His golden rays lighten our hearts,
We run and play in his light.

Give praise to God for sister Moon
And every twinkling star;
They shine in heaven, bright and clear
And watch us from afar.

Give praise to God for brother Wind,
Who brings the storms and showers;
Rushing, whirling, racing round,
Drenching trees and flowers.

Give praise to God for sister Water,
Needed for all we do;
She quenches our thirst and makes us clean,
Refreshing us anew.

Give praise to God for brother Fire,
At once both wild and tame;
Keeping us warm and safe from harm,
But still a mighty flame.

Give praise to God for mother Earth,
Who supports us with her love;
She feeds us with her fruits and herbs,
Sent from heaven above.

Based on 'The Canticle of the Sun', St Francis of Assisi

$\mathcal{D}$ay is done,
Sun is gone,
From the hills,
From the sky.

Safely rest,
Gently dream,
Without fear,
God is near.

Father, we thank you for the night,
And for the pleasant morning light;
For rest and food and loving care,
And all that makes the day so fair.

Help us to do the things we should,
To be to others kind and good;
In all we do, in work or play,
To grow more loving every day.

Rebecca Weston

Now as I lie down to sleep,
I pray, Lord, that my soul you'll keep;
May you guard me through the night
And wake me with the morning light.

Angels bless and angels keep,
Angels guard me while I sleep.
Bless my heart and bless my home,
Bless my spirit as I roam.
Guide and guard me through the night,
And wake me with the morning light.

God, our family is here.
Thank you for our home,
For the love that unites us,
For the peace we had today,
For the hope we have for tomorrow,
For our health, our work,
   our food and the bright sky,
Which make us happy;
And for all our friends everywhere.

Based on 'Lord, behold our family here assembled',
Robert Louis Stevenson

God in heaven hear my prayer,
Keep me in your loving care.
Be my guide in all I do,
Bless all those who love me too.

The verses in this book are versions of
traditional prayers, unless otherwise stated.

First published in German as
Ein Engel beschütze dich! by Alfred Hahn's Verlag,
Esslinger Verlag J.F. Schreiber in 2009
First published in English by Floris Books in 2013
© 2009 Alfred Hahn's Verlag
Illustrations © Art & Design Licensing/Antje Jentsch
English version © Floris Books 2013

British Library CIP data available
ISBN 978-178250-004-9
Printed in Malaysia